THE DETAILZ OF RETAIL

105 Lessons Missing From the Associate Training Manual

Markesha G. Tatum

Copyright © 2016 Markesha G. Tatum

All rights reserved.

ISBN: 0692688048
ISBN-13: 978-0692688045 (GEM Publishing)

The Detailz In Retail

DEDICATION

The Tatums, Grants, Waters:
without your support, I could not have completed this project.

R. Tatum – Thank you for letting me live my dreams!

Dominique – Thank you for all of your assistance: writing, reading and advising.

Aamira– Just because

Roxann D.– Thanks for the encouragement and stories.

CONTENTS

Acknowledgments	i
Introduction	ii
Part 1: The Customers	1
Part 2: The Criminals	94
Part 3: The Sales Associates	110
Part 4: The Management	146

Editing and Proofreading Services

Provided by Bonniejean Alford.

Bonniejean Alford is a writer, editor, researcher and social media guru holding two Master of Art degrees (Sociology and Communication). Through her company, Alford Enterprises, she provides clients with a variety of specialty communication services aimed at enhancing quality and brand messaging. Ms. Alford is dedicated to meeting her clients' communication, public relations, and marketing needs with excellence at an affordable cost, no matter their industry. She works with clients in all areas of the globe, including Australia, Ireland, Europe, and Asia. Ms. Alford resides in Illinois with her husband.

Visit her website at **www.alfordenterprises.net**

ACKNOWLEDGMENTS

Retail Friends:

K.M, E.P., E.C., R.V., T.P., J.F., S.H. – Thank you for the laughs, guidance, support, and friendship.

Introduction

What you are about to read is not only entertaining but also provides a brief examination of human behavior and the internal conflicts within each of us, especially as it is related in the retail world. The Detailz of Retail provides scenarios with lessons store employees should take from the situation to make them a better retail associate. We are all human; some have extreme emotional issues, while others are delightful and pleasant – and anywhere in between. Written as a catharsis for dealing with different personalities on a daily basis, this book shows that you can learn to become the strong and flexible retail associate needed to creatively and tactfully navigate through the day. My goal is to train and enlighten retailers about the ordeals their associates encounter. This book is meant to serve as a teaching tool for individuals new to the retail industry, providing lessons in empathy, especially for district and store managers to assist with an attitude of 'think-before-you-hire'. Most importantly, the lessons serve as tools to guide associates as they deal with their customers.

While the focus in The Detailz of Retail is to train associates through true stories and some laughter, customers can also benefit from these lessons. The stories are not meant as an attack of any kind, but rather a reality check into the ins and outs of retail. They can help customers have an enjoyable shopping experience. And maybe, just maybe, it will help some customers 'think-before-they-shop', creating a better experience for everyone involved. Sit back and enjoy the stories while you learn the lessons. And remember, it is okay to laugh – just not in front of the customers.

PART I
THE CUSTOMERS

<u>The Compulsive Shopper</u>

The compulsive shopper, also known as the shop-a-holic, enters the store with an air of awe and ooh. Examines each and every fabric while she quizzes the sales associate's knowledge on every detail from the hem to the neckline. The fitting room has been started as our queen continues to peruse the store. At this point, she believes the associates are her personal shoppers and demands their full attention of all associates regardless of others shopping. The queen has tried on every style in every color. She is satisfied and overly excited with her selections. Her majesty makes it to the cash register to wrap up and suddenly spots a 'to die for' bracelet! The transaction is nearly completed before she saunters off for round two.

Our queen is about to embark upon the excuses and justification phase. Pieces have been selected for so and so's birthday, wedding, graduation, and/or any other occasion on the calendar. The queen questions her selections but does not eliminate one single item: *when in doubt, stop talkin' and keep on walkin'*. Every article on the receipt had been justified and reinforced by the sales associate before leaving the store. She had gladly pulled out her credit card, swiping with exhilaration. She thanks all of her loyal subjects for assisting her, murmurs a thank you to the fashion gods for making the experience possible, and leaves the store on cloud nine. Ironically, you may find that the compulsive shopper just happens to be an employee of the retailer.

Lesson: Treat this customer well, without breaking any rules of course. They come in often and spend a lot of money, which is a win for the company and the customer.

<u>The Indecisive Shopper</u>

The indecisive shopper shares some similarities with our compulsive shopper. The indecisive shopper will try on the latest pieces and admire the new trends as she glances and prances in the mirror. She'll analyze and question why she should purchase a particular item and do a little dance called, "I like it but…I don't know if I should get this" or "I really like this, do you like it?" This diabolical dialogue will carry on for more than fifteen minutes as the associate prays for an interruption from this madness; the shopper is pretty sure the associate went to check their phone for missed calls or texts. The associate returns to our shopper to see if a choice has been made: lo and behold, *NO* choice was made. In fact, the customer has left the fitting room to look for more pieces to add to the discussion of, "Should I purchase". The indecisive shopper will spend an exceedingly long time in the fitting room trying to decide on what to get and why to get it.

Much like the compulsive shopper, they too, began to justify why they should make the purchase. Unlike the compulsive shopper, the indecisive shopper will make a phone call as if it were their lifeline and ask for reinforcement in making a decision prior to leaving the wardrobe room. Unlike the rush our compulsive shopper receives as she swipes her credit card, the indecisive shopper will inquire about the exact details of the return policy, if, in fact, she is not already familiar with each store's policy. The indecisive shopper will come back the next day and return the items, appearing hesitant while making the return. Could it be that this process is a part of a psychotherapy assignment, yet not retail therapy!

Lesson: Be honest and helpful with this customer. Give feedback to questions, without trying to rush them through the process. Don't ignore other customers though.

The Self-Esteem Booster

Customer: "Are you sure this looks good?" "Am I too fat? I look fat in this." "Let me try on the other color in the same size." "Okay, let me try the other color in a size bigger."

Customer: "Ohm, can you bring me the first color I tried, I think I like that size it fits better."
"The xx-small is acting as if she's an extra-large."

Customer: "I can't decide."

Associate: "You look great!" Just smile, always smile.

Customer: "Thank you!"

Lesson: Just go with it. Nothing can be said to this customer. The help she requires is above your pay grade. Do not try to reason with this customer. All an associate can say is, "You look great!" But remember not to lie to the customer. Try something a seven year old would say, "I don't think this is going to work for you. Try this (*another item in hand. Always be prepared with an alternative*) instead." The worst thing you can do is tell them they look great when they don't. Your honesty may actually help them leave more quickly.

It's A Blouse Not A Foreign Policy Memo

Have you ever seen someone examine a piece of clothing for five minutes? Some customers are retired seamstresses or tailors and some just think they are. Upon meeting these 'experts', be prepared to discuss the stitching of the hemline and type of fabric used. The 'experts' will also share with you their dreams of becoming a designer and how they would have designed the garment differently. Those stories are delightful and warmhearted. In addition to the 'experts', you may encounter the shopper that is looking for something critical to say and want to appear to be 'experts'. This 'expert' will examine the garment in such detail as if they were going to submit the item to the United Nations. They will purchase the item after expecting a discount for its flaws, only to return again the next week and go through the same process: examine the garment, criticize the garment, criticize the designer, and then purchase. Thank you, see you next time!

Lesson: Make sure they don't try and damage the item to get an extra discount.

The Return Policy Challenger

The return policy challenger is very familiar with the return policy but will often feel the need to force, entice, and bully the sales associate to break the rules. Often you will hear phrases such as, "Can you just do it for me this one time?" and "I promise I will bring my receipt next time" (*Next time? You mean there will be a next time?*). If it's the indecisive shopper making the return, she may say, "Well, I cut the tags off because I thought I was going to wear it but I decided to return the item. I swear it's not worn" or "I don't usually do this" (*Are you kidding me? You were just here last week!*)

Another type of return challenger is the lady who holds onto items for five years and decides not to keep the items. (*Lady, this is not a Chanel suit, it is so out of style*). The receipt is folded and slightly faded in currier font. The funny thing about the over two year returns is that you get to walk down memory lane. For example, as you are checking the date you may think to yourself as you examine the items, "Yes, paisley print was popular in 2003." The memory alone is proof that the return is not legit. Another entertaining aspect of the over two year returns are the often quoted phrases, "I wasn't sure if I liked it or not" (*It took you five years to decide if you liked something! Next time, maybe donate to a charity instead.*)

"The Customer is always right!" Yeah, about that...Most times customers are just wrong, all day long, WRONG! Inside out, upside down WRONG. Even if as an associate you have to smile and not actually say they are wrong, politely imply it.

Lesson: Have a complete understanding of the return policy. Call your manager to make any decisions about exceptions to the rule.

The Dirty Returns

The return of dirty items has got to be one of the biggest blows to a sales associate's intelligence! "We all wear clothes, we know what they look like worn!" For some reason, a customer will bring in worn garments and attempt to return to the store. Perhaps the customer thinks the sales associate resides in Dumbville with a house built on sand and are too dumbfounded to recognize a worn item. Whatever the case, it is tacky to even attempt returning already worn items, unless it is truly a problem with the product.

One lady had worn her sweater to a dinner party, snagged it, got marinara sauce on it, and shared the entire story about the lovely dinner party she and her husband attended in the city. Sounds okay so far, well, she claims her husband noticed the snag in the sweater (*less than a millimeter*) and thought she should return the sweater. Initially, the woman only stated she had worn the item but insisted it was not snagged. The marinara stains were apparent and invalidated her reason for returning. Nice try.

Lesson: Check for snags in all garments. All sales aren't good sales. If you sell an item with the knowledge of the slightest imperfection, it will only bite you in the butt when the customer returns the item. Ethics and honesty should proceed any sale.

The Naughty Pants

This one lady tried to return a pair of pants with grass stains and the associate said to her, "There is not a free trial on clothes."

Lesson: Thoroughly check the items before you process the return. Associates, humble yourself and politely state the return policy. Try not to laugh, especially while customers are in earshot.

Toys

Every possible scenario for returning items is not just limited to women. One gentleman decided to try and return a box of Legos. The only thing that ruined his nice little plan of deception: he forgot to count the pieces. The clerk emptied the box and found only four pieces, then asked the man to explain why there are only four out of one hundred pieces left? When asked what happened the man' response was, "I guess my son did not put the pieces back in the box." The gentleman left the store. Can you believe he tried to return four out of 100 hundred pieces?

Lesson: Check the box and inform customers not to entrust your kids with the details of packing up an item when it comes to returning a toy they like. Unfortunately, you never know a person's circumstance, so don't be too judgmental – it could actually be an honest mistake.

The Green Outfit That Had An Herbal Essence

Two girls and guy came in the store and made a purchase. It didn't appear as if they were going to make a purchase but they did *want* something to *take* with them. After about an hour in the store, one of the girls purchased a green track suit. A few days later, the girl that made the purchase came back by herself to return the track suit. Upon inspecting the items being returned, one couldn't help but notice a strong stench coming from the item. The customer stared through noticeably red eyes as the associate checked the item again. After being informed that her item can't be returned due to the strong odor, the customer, of course, appeared shocked and stated that maybe she should hurry up and leave the shopping center. Now, why would she want to leave the center immediately? I guess she was feeling a little paranoid about the odor coming from the item. It is a shame that some shoppers don't know they shouldn't burn, blow and return. A little Febreeze goes a long way.

Lesson: Pay attention to the behavior of your customers and kill them with kindness. Follow your store's loss prevention guidelines in case you suspect a customer might be engaging in something illegal.

The Other Black Dress

The other black dress incident occurred on a Saturday afternoon. Every now and then the entitled customer can get a bit snobbish and snooty and this day was a definite case of Miss Snooty-Pooty. An associate was in the process of accepting the return of a dress but noticed several chalky stains throughout the outside of the dress. The associate called a manager over to assist. The manager gave a thumbs down on the return and the associate proceeded to tell the customer.

The customer was not happy about the denial of her return. She blamed the stains on her kids and their friends. Claimed she did not know where the stains came from and how the store should be able to get the stains out without it involving her. Customer then proceeded to call her mother and express her contempt. Customer stated she went to law school and then proceeded to pull out her wallet, quite expensive with a recognizable logo. As she is holding her wallet, she begins to insult the associate and manager by saying, "my wallet cost..." The manager flashed a warning glance to the customer before she said something she was going to regret. The customer realized she should retreat from her insult, take her dress, and leave, gathering her things in a hasty manner.

They wished that was the last of her but two weeks later they learned that was not the end of Little Miss Snooty-Pooty. Little Miss entitled Snooty-Pooty brought in ten items from another store to return out of spite. Apparently, Little Miss Snooty-Pooty didn't have much of a life. If only those with more expendable wealth would not demean others life would be grand. This lady's behavior was disgusting.

Lesson: Be aware of the Snooty-Pootie, don't' become a Snooty-Pooty, and don't allow Snooty-

Pooty to lower your morale. Even though Snooty-Pooty's wallet was expensive, she still didn't have enough money to buy good manners, humility, or empathy.

<u>Last But Not Clean</u>

Ladies, please dry-clean your items before you attempt to return a worn and dirty item. The ultimate and most disgusting return occurred when a young lady between nineteen and twenty-four brought in a dress. She pretended to be interested in exchanging the item (*yeah, go through the motions, make the sales associate think you are at least trying to find something.*)…"Okay, now that I have pretended to look interested in another item, it's time to mosey on to the register." She presented an item for return with a very popular style and cut;

can't beat an A-line (*a girl's best friend next to spandex*). Meanwhile, the cashier proceeds with the return; usual questions, "why are you returning this item?" The response, "I didn't like it." (*"How do you not like this dress?"*) Note that it is very difficult to check an item over while another customer insists on being nominated, "the most rude and distracting person of the evening."

Back to the dress return…well, since the other customer desperately needed attention a thorough inspection of the dress was not executed properly. The refund was given. The customer left and the cashier proceeded to look at the garment. A thorough inspection was made of the Dress.

You know when something doesn't feel right, go with it! Out of all the returns thus far, this had to be the most appalling and unnecessary. After turning the dress inside out (*brace yourself*) to the associate's utter surprise, there it was, a streak of white chalk-like stain that can only be found from the anatomy of the female persuasion. Unnecessary and disgusting. Quite frankly, if a customer must return a dress that has been worn, hopefully they will spend the extra ten dollars and have the item dry cleaned, not returning it in this condition. Truthfully, it is never okay, or cute, to return worn merchandise. It is unethical and disgusting…and customers who do this will not be forgotten, known as the "dirty dress lady."

Lesson: Never allow yourself to be distracted by another associate or customer while processing a return. Call your manager from the office and ask for assistance. Once the customer is gone, you are stuck explaining the dirty dress and no one wants to have that discussion. The only exception to the rule of returning worn clothing is in the case of a true defect in the product – but even then the item should be cleaned before making the return.

What Would You Do If I Threw A Tantrum And Demand You Accept My Return?

You must be thinking, "What three year old walks into a store and threatens to throw a tantrum?" Well folks, this person was a mature adult female. This customer came to return a damaged accessory without a receipt. The origin of the items is unknown: stolen, found, purchase date, sale-priced, or full-priced. The woman insisted she was not the type of person to be dishonest (by the way, they all say that). The customer had the store's return policy explained to her. She refused to accept a store credit for her return and then asked what would the Big Wheelers say if told a customer threw a tantrum?

Speechless, the associate just looked at the woman (*imagine squinting eyes with head slightly tilted to the right: "I know its Friday but is this really happening?"*). It was unbelievable that this woman insisted she wasn't the dishonest 'type' yet she insisted that the associate act in a dishonest manner by breaking store policy for her returned items. Must have been just fine, as long as it wasn't on her conscience?

Lesson: Be aware of sweet elderly ladies that are prepared to throw tantrums. This lady has had many years of practice on getting her way. There is nothing anyone between the ages of 18-35 can tell her. Call your manager immediately for assistance. This situation is above your pay grade.

Can't Handle Problems (*Never Work In Retail*)

"I can't handle problems" was a true statement made by a woman who wished to return three half pound necklaces. One and half pounds may not seem like a lot but this woman was at least in her late sixties. The associate began to question the woman about the return to make sure that she knew that they were to be worn separately and not as a group. She went on to explain that she was aware and thought it was cute and trendy regardless of the neck and shoulder safety. When asked if she wanted to keep one which would be easier to wear, she said in a nasty tone that she didn't want to keep one and just didn't want any problems. The associate reassured her that she just wanted to make sure before the return was complete and then the woman stated, "I can't handle problems, as you can see!" The associate was at a loss for words for two seconds, finally responding kindly by saying, "I don't think anyone welcomes problems, but I hope you find the necklace that suits your vision." The transaction completed, the customer apologized for her attitude and thanked the associate for all of the help and concern.

Lesson: Empathy.

The Bread Lady

A customer shopping in grocery store accused the bagger of smashing her bread. The lady got upset and balled up the bread and threw it at the cashier and asked if they like smashed bread.

Lesson: Don't try to calm the customer down, seek a manager and possibly security.

The Barter System

Once upon a time, in a place so far away, there was this system called, "bartering". If you are an entrepreneur, then you are very much familiar with the term and its function in the community and business world. For those of you who are not, bartering is kind of like give-and-take, swapping of services. For example, you give someone a barrel of apples and they will give you three dozens of eggs.

Although, this may seem archaic, there are a lot of business owners who still participate in this type of networking. A great system but why do women (*and some men*) think they can enter a store, a clothing store in the mall, as if they were a vendor at a farmer's market? A chain clothing store is under corporate guidelines, why do they think bartering is an option for discounts?

There is a woman that comes into a particular store at least once a week. This woman will make her way around the store, selects her pieces, tries them on, and make her way to the cash register for purchase. Now, this barter lady is no dummy. Barter lady has calculated every last digit and detail of the items. She is aware of the price and has prepared her speech, right amount of eye contact, and most importantly the piece of clothing she is willing to part with if she is unable to negotiate the 'right' price. As she reaches the register, she's talking about how well the store is doing, discusses possible layoffs at her job, and so forth. Then, as all of the items get processed, she leans over and whispers, "Oh, come on just give me a discount. Can you just knock off another twenty percent? Oh, you can do it!" The barter lady continues her swan song with, "I promise I will come back and buy more!" And the famous line, "Can you do it just this one time?" The cashier politely states, "No, ma'am, I can never just give a discount for the fun of it? Can me and my family come and live with you after I lose my job for giving you twenty percent off of your purchase, just this one time?"

After many attempts to intimidate and plead, the woman leaves the store with one item less than what she had arrived with at the counter.

Lesson: In bartering situations, it is wise for the cashier not to negotiate their integrity, which means understanding your customer's budget by assisting with more functional and stylish options that are within their budget. In the end, the cashier is still employed and the customer is still a stylish recessionista!

Holiday-Turns Into Holi-Don't

This next situation takes place in a main stream department store during the holiday season. Picture it, a day in the city, cold and windy, a wedding is scheduled to take place soon, kids are running, babies are screaming, mothers are yelling, in-laws are scorning (*you spoil your child*), and employees are not too jolly because the Christmas bonus was nothing but a carrot. One customer was looking for an item on a bridal registry list. She wandered about aimlessly searching for the item but no luck; then went to ask an employee for assistance, thinking this would alleviate her of the pressure in finding the item in the store. The employee was obviously overwhelmed and yelled, "I can't do this!" The customer was stunned and thought, "Is it Whine-o'clock yet? It's definitely wine-o'clock for me now!"

Lesson: This lesson is definitely an important lesson for any salesperson to learn. Remember where you are and do your best. Excuse yourself when it is becoming too much. Call your manager and ask to leave for a few minutes. If you are really in tune with yourself, simply take a deep breath and understand that you can't save the world but you can do your job and go home.

The Final Sale Explanation

Customer: "What if I buy it today and it doesn't fit my friend, can I bring it back tomorrow?"

Associate: "No, the item is a final sale."

Customer: "If she can't fit it, I can't bring it back?"

Associate: "No, the item can't be returned."

Customer: "But if my friend can't fit it, I have to return it."

Associate: "All final sale items cannot be returned even if it doesn't fit. I encourage you to send your friend in to try it on for herself or give the item to someone else."

Customer: "So, I cannot return the item?"

Associate: "That is correct."

Lesson: In order to bypass this circle of nonsense you have to do your best to make sure that customer does not see or purchase a final sale item. Talk her out of it. Whisper quietly in her ear and tell her that the price is too high or the item is damaged and out of season. If this item is sold to the customer above, you can best believe that item will be back two days later with a sob story to follow. Save yourself the time and effort. Remember, not all sales are good sales. Maintain integrity and sanity.

Scanner As A Weapon

There are some items that just can't be returned. Non-returnable items are the ones that touch the unmentionable areas like: the va-jj (coined by a character/writer on *Grey's Anatomy*) and the peeping pipe. One day a gentlemen brought in a queen sized sheet set that had clearly been used. The package was opened and the sheets appeared to be used. The gentleman was informed that the store would be unable to process his return and explained the reason why. The gentleman became highly agitated and demanded his item be returned. Again, the gentleman was reminded of why and told no. The gentleman continues to escalate and causes a scene (*no longer acting like a gentleman*). The angry man was asked to leave and prior to doing so, the angry man grabbed the scanner and hit the cashier in the forehead with the scanner.

If you are unfamiliar with a scanner, picture a mini gun detached from its base. The angry man was TOLD to leave. Makes you wonder, was violence the answer? Who was the real victim: the customer demanding the return or the cashier who got hit on the forehead? Some people just want to enjoy the thrill of pulling a fast one but some people really need their money back for whatever reason: to feed their family, gas (*we all know how high the gas has been*), or medicine. You never know what a person is going through so don't make assumptions. At the same time, there are rules and guidelines that you agreed to follow when you took the job.

Lesson: Call the manager. The situation is above your pay rate

Penny Pinchers

Gotta love the penny pinchers. The penny pincher is worse than the grandma who saves for a thousand rainy days. Penny pinchers enjoy a little style. The penny pincher will have you check the price three times on the same item hoping it will magically change to the price they are willing to buy the item. The pincher will bring every coupon to use on one purchase even though it clearly states, "Cannot be combined with other offers," the standard coupon clause. Not only will they bring in a dozen coupons, the coupons are for other stores.

The penny pincher will try on the item, hold on tightly to the item and as the purchase is being made, they will insist that the store is too expensive but she loves the brand. Penny pincher will also go to the sale rack and switch out the tags from a sale item and attach it to a full priced item as if the associates are not familiar with the merchandise. The penny pincher will appear shocked and say, "I love that blouse, is there a discount I can have?" The penny pincher also collects free items like hangers and perfume samples. She needs to leave knowing she got something for nothing.

Lesson: Learn to love your penny pinchers. Call her when there's a sale that she can combine with a coupon. She will always come to you. If you take the time to get to know them, they will offer you good advice and life lessons. Respect her hustle.

Oh, Honey Please Call Me For Sales

Customer: "Oh, Hun, call me when this goes on sale."

Associate: "It's on a promotion now at 40% off."

Customer: "Call me when it goes on sale more. Can I get a water?" (*She meant five waters for her entire crew*).

Customer: "Honey, can you track this down for me at another store?" As she holds her phone up displaying an item from last season.

Associate: "Yes, I'll let you know if we find it."

Customer: "Can I get some perfume samples?"

Associate: "Sure, here's a couple."

"Oh, can they all have some too?" (*They implied five kids and one more adult*).

Lesson: Avoid too much contact by showing her everything that's not on sale. She'll grow weary of you and leave on her own accord. The entire experience is exhausting, to say the least. No one has time for energy moochers.

Entitlement Issues

The entitled shopper is a unique individual. She requires a certain type of personality to assist her. The entitled shopper is similar to our compulsive shopper. She will assume you are there for her and only her! She will attempt to order you around and this is why she requires an associate who will be able to remind her of the mere fact that we are human beings and you are at the mall not on the set of <u>The Princess Diaries</u> (*Me, starring Me*). An associate with the right personality will be able to convey the rules to our shopper in a tactful manner. As the shopper/associate rules of conduct are established the shopping can begin. The entitled shopper will want every discount and make not so subtle reminders that she spends an enormous amount of money on the brand.

Lesson: The entitled shopper is exhausting because she doesn't hear the word no, it's not available, or it's on hold. As the associate, you need to remain strong and not allow the customer to mentally exhaust you. Somewhere along the way, someone did not teach this person the art of empathy.

The "I Don't Like My Body Today" Shopper

Oh, My Goodness! Not this again. "I don't like my body today" shopper is one of the least favorite types of customers. No matter how great they may look and how much you tell them how great they look, she will continue to tell you how she shouldn't be there shopping and nothing looks good. Finally, after attempting to beat a dead horse, you concede and advise her to return on day she is feeling better. "I don't like my body today" shoppers are, in fact, the women with the most ideal body types. Occasionally, you may see the new mom or mother of two and the second birth was not good to her at all (*after the third pregnancy, moms have accepted the labor of love baby fat*).

Lesson: Be mindful and empathetic of the customer with self-image issues. Usually, there's more underlying issues that has nothing to do with you, therefore you can't really do much other than make them feel less anxious while shopping. However, bear in mind, you are not a psychotherapist. Don't create a situation that's above your pay grade. Since this is a serious topic and you will encounter a number of young girls and women with self-image issues, you should visit www.nationaleatingdisorders.org to become more familiar with these types of issues.

After-The-Fact Price Adjusters

The after-the-fact price adjusters share qualities with the penny pinchers and the entitled shopper. The after-the-fact price adjusters will appear in the store with a two week old purchase of sale items and a current coupon they recently received in the mail. This is where the entitled shopper will create a scene if she is not granted an adjustment or while the policy is being explained. You may hear a phrase such as, "I don't get this at other stores" (right, of course you don't). Then the speech about the economy and how she would like to save money is slowly coming. *("The economy? Helllooo, I'm under paid, working retail").*

If only shoppers would stop trying to bully associates into breaking policies.

Lesson: Make sure you have a clear idea on the current promotions and know the return policy like the back of your hand. You don't deserve to be yelled at by anybody. If you are being yelled at, quickly figure out if you need to adjust your body language or tone or call your manager. Try to keep the peace but still uphold the company policy. Check with your manager and understand their return style. Some managers like to avoid situations and will always honor the customer's request; some never will. Clearly, that is at the discretion of the manager and that is what they are paid to do. Managers should be clear with associates where they stand on price adjustments and returns especially if it is going against store policy.

Gift Boxes

Gift boxes are a hot commodity. Everyone wants a gift box even for items they didn't purchase in your store. Gift boxes usually contain the store's logo which gives more value to the gift. The giver is validated by choosing a gift and taking the time to wrap it in a coordinating box. One customer came into the store and purchased one small item. After the purchase, she asked for several boxes. The sales associate was puzzled for two reasons: 1) why did the customer need a box for the item purchased? 2) And why is she asking for several boxes? The associate decided to verbalize her questions.

Associate: "Ma'am, our smallest box would be a bit large for the item you purchased."

Customer: "It's okay. Can you wrap it?"

Associate: "Sure. I can only give boxes for the items you purchased today."

Customer: "I didn't get any boxes the last time I was here and I got a lot of stuff" (*No, she didn't.*)

Associate: "Oh, okay." (*Not really okay, but why engage in a power struggle.*)

This same customer came in three months later and requested ten gift boxes (*without a purchase*) because the store didn't have any in stock at the time of her last purchase.

Lesson: Gift boxes are important for customers even if they don't make a purchase, but giving them out too freely will affect the store's profits and loss budget. While it is true that a customer shouldn't have to worry about a manger having to explain the expenses to their boss, clear policies should be created and followed by the store. Find a balance between giving the customer what they want and not allowing the store be taken advantage. Within reason, the boxes do serve as a form of advertising as it builds good will with a customer.

Expired Coupons: Why Can't I Use It?

The coupon cutter shopped her little heart out and made it to the register. After bagging the items and nearly completing the transaction, she pulls out a coupon. The coupon doesn't look familiar at all. The associate carefully reads the coupon and discovers that it's been expired for a year. The customer says, "Why can't I use it?" The cashier explains for the second time that the coupon is no longer valid. Customer continues by saying, "So, I can't use it?"

Lesson: Pay attention to coupons and always have something for your favorite customers. They will come back to you many times even without a coupon just because you were considerate of their budget. Ask your customer to leave their email or phone number so that you can call them for promotions and sales. Most retailers encourage you to create a customer data base for your store. If not, you should start one on your own to increase your sales and rapport.

This Isn't A Daycare And I'm Not The Nanny!

Some parents assume that all stores are like Ikea and have a built-in daycare. Well, they don't. Attention all parents please control your children upon entering the store please. Explain the rules so that they will behave accordingly. Remember your kids are only cute to you. There is nothing appealing about a child running around the store disrupting other shoppers. Also, bear in mind, that the store is not child proofed.

Now, here's a true story. One day a mother and daughter entered the store. The daughter began running around, crawling back and forth underneath the tables. Guess what happens next? Yep, the little child acting like a monkey bumped her head (*because we didn't see that coming*). And, have you already guessed what happens next? Yep, you guessed it. The mother of the child behaving like a monkey had the nerve to blame the store for not child proofing the edges of the tables. In the midst of the child's tears, an associate was sent to get ice.

The associate retrieving the ice had to be creative and scrape ice out of the freezer of the mini fridge to make an ice pack since one wasn't readily available. Why she didn't get the first aid kit, no one knows.

***Lesson*:** Parents should absolutely watch their kids and associates should not have to remind parents of this. Make sure you know where to find the first aid kit and how to use the contents. Maybe request your manager or HR provide you with training.

Demolition Girl

If you thought the story above was unbelievable, brace yourself and pay close attention to the next tale. They called her the tag girl. A girl and her mother are walking around browsing. Sounds okay so far, right? As the mother continues to browse, the child continues to walk slowly behind the mother. Little by little, the following distance between mother and child increased. And with this distance, the little girl took full advantage of this grand opportunity to begin the "removal" of the price tags. The little girl was given the stink-eye by the associates as they re-attached each price tag that was removed. The little girl continued until the mother finally decided to make a purchase and realized she had a child with her. The associates continued with the stink-eye but the little girl couldn't care less.

Lesson: Parents should discipline their kids. It's absolutely not okay for parents to allow their children to misbehave in stores or destroy property. In some cases, you may have to give the kid the "stink eye" especially if the parents aren't doing anything. Moreover, you have to maintain a safe environment within the store. This may involve politely reminding a parent to keep track of their child. Worst case, you have to ask the parent and their child to leave. Safety is more important than a sale any day of the week.

Little Shopper In Training

Don't let your daughter, or in some cases your son, try it if you are not going to buy it.

How many of you have heard the before entering the store threat from your parents: "When we go inside the store, DON'T TOUCH ANYTHING" which is accompanied by "DON'T ASK FOR ANYTHING" Well, some parents are firm believers in the before-you-enter-the-store speech/threat. But often times, the prepping took place before leaving the car, forgotten long before actually entering the store. And not everyone adheres to the "Don't touch" pre-shopping mantra. Also, some children enjoy a challenge, especially in public places. For instance, the de-tagger girl was banging a perfume bottle on the glass table and then began to spray the table with perfume. The de-tagger girl required a special kind of handling. The de-tagger was so annoying that she annoyed another kid in the store.

Lesson: These future shoppers need respect, yes, but not at the expense of the store. It is completely okay to lose a sale to their parent if protecting the rest of the merchandise or other customers. Try to work with the parent to make the situation a win for both them and the store. Invest in a pack of unisex stickers to hand out when kids are behaving and to encourage appropriate behavior.

Emotional Baggage

When you hear the phrase, "emotional baggage" many might automatically think of a person in a relationship, but maybe not. Many associates never think they would have to calm someone down while shopping as the customer freaked out over the selections of clothing. The customer wanted a specific look, but did not know what that look was or how to express her desires in a proper adult manner. After her emotional outburst, tears and all, she was able to look at the fashionable pieces that were offered to her and found that they were quite stylish (*maybe an adult tantrum department with a few time-out chairs is needed*).

As the customer collected herself, she says, "I am so sorry! You're only trying to help me and I'm being a total bitch to you!" (*Yes, you are!*). She continues to say, "This is probably why my life if so messed up and why my relationships aren't working. It's because of my attitude!" (*Ya think! Associates really don't get paid enough for this*). The styling session ended with her appearing happy about her selections. Side note, this lady is also known for wearing and returning, so the associate made a mental note of all the pieces and prepared for the "attempt to return" visit!

Six months later, the return visit takes place. Well, it was a waste of photographic memory data because she was ahead of the game and brought in a purchase from another store to return. The excuse was, the skirt was defective because the hem fell out while it was being worn. The skirt actually looked as if it had the time of its life for a lifetime. Not the average eight hour work day look. (*What exactly is that company paying her to do?*) She continues to explain in a highly emotional manner (*we are all aware of the emotional baggage lady*) that she had to return the blouse (worn) because she couldn't wear it with anything else. Now, the problem: The blouse was stained to no end! (*Maybe wear a bib or a smock*). Yes, she threw a tantrum when she heard the evil phrase, "We cannot accept this item" (the blouse). All hell broke loose. Associates may love their job, but this is ludicrous and unacceptable behavior!

The customer is always right? Not in this case.

Lesson: Smile and calmly explain you are not authorized to handle this return, and then call the manager. Do not attempt to deal with this customer. Maybe instead, call security.

Heart Attack

Prior to the gift box requests, the same customer entered the store to return a pair of shoes. The shoes were obviously not purchased for her because they were too small. The customer purchased the shoes for her sister but the sister didn't like them. Unfortunately, the receipt for the item had expired and they could not be returned. Well, the customer could not handle the denial and began to fake a heart attack. She was offered water and a chair to sit in and relax. The customer did not want the paramedics called. The manager quietly told the customer that she would speak with the district manager on her behalf. The customer felt much better hearing this offer. The heart wants what it wants.

Lesson: Medical situations do arise. In those legitimate cases, the customer has no choice but to accept your assistance and call the paramedics – you aren't a medical professional after all, how do you know for sure if they are faking. If in doubt, it may be best to contact your manager and have them handle it. Do your best to calm the situation while you wait.

The Unrealistic Request

The middle of November. The temperature is about 50 degrees or less, the wind is howling in the night. During this time, winter coats and cashmere are selling out fast. Wool pants and thick denim are flying off the racks. Now, imagine a cozy fireplace and hot chocolate permeate your mind and you can't wait to get home. As you're standing around at work in the middle of November, you're not really expecting what is about to happen next,

Customer: "Do you have any short black shorts?"

Associate: "No, we don't have any shorts right now" (*While standing next to a table full of sweaters*). "We probably won't get any until early spring."

The customer's next question, "Do you have black skirts?"

Associate: "Well, here is a black skirt. It sits about two inches above the knee."

Customer: "Do you have something that's shorter?"

"Are you kidding me? That's like going into Lane Bryant and asking if they carry a double zero." (*"I'm sorry we don't carry hoochie gear"*).

The women who shop here can barely tolerate sleeveless tops showing that fabulous flab. The associate suggested she might find what she was looking for at Forever Young. Clearly, she was doing something at the last minute or she was sent in there on a dare. Now, that makes perfect sense.

Lesson: Just try and do your best to meet their needs. Don't try to sell them something they don't want. Don't be afraid to refer customers to another store to get the item they need that you may not carry. It will build trust and they will be back for the items you do carry that they want or need.

Ummnn

Customer: "If I return a pair of shoes that I purchased with a store credit, can I get cash back?"

(*Ummnn, NO!*)

Associate: "No, you will receive a store credit."

Customer: "Why?"

Associate: "You will receive a store credit because that was how the original transaction was tendered."

Customer: "Okay, but I don't understand why"

Just keep smiling. Just keep smiling. Just keep smiling.

***Lesson*:** Exercise patience. Know the store policy and the laws of your state because you will get a customer that may know more than you and you want to be prepared.

Woe Is Me

Have you ever met someone who makes you their best friend in less than five minutes? In those five minutes you learn what they really think about the people in their lives. For instance, one customer talked so much about her mother-in-law that she made Jane Fonda's character in Monster-in-law appear like a sweet angel. The wardrobe room is the most popular place for the action to happen.

***Lesson*:** Listen as best you can. You have a job to do. If needed, apologize and step away. Check in on the customer from time to time, letting them know they haven't been forgotten and their needs matter, but you have other duties to attend to as well.

Not My Size

"Do you have anyone working that's a size fourteen?" said in front of the size two sales associate, who's young and perplexed by the question. Speechless, in fact.

"I think a size fourteen would understand and be able to better help me."

The size six manager overheard and responds, "Sorry, ma'am but we do not. However, all of our associates are equipped, knowledgeable, honest, and able to assist anyone." Size six was accepted.

Lesson: Recognizing your customer's needs is important, but know your store's limits. Reassurance is really what most customers are looking for anyway, so be positive, honest, and help the best you can.

<u>The Tactless Request</u>

Customer: "Can you give me your discount?"

Associate: "No, that's against store policy."

Just keep smiling, just keep smiling, and just keep smiling.

Lesson: Don't lose your job to help a stranger save a few bucks. But if you have a few spare coupons laying around, and your manager is okay with it, feel free to offer one to the customer.

The Delusional And Notorious Zipper Breaker

The delusional and notorious zipper breaker comes in the store at least twice a week. This particular young lady works at another retailer and demands all of our attention. She insists on trying on clothes that are too small for her which results in her breaking the zipper. In addition to damaging the product, she will look at a handbag, place it on hold and come back a day later only to place it on hold again. She finally decides that she wants to purchase the handbag.

The associates think they're done with her until she comes back to return the handbag that has clearly been used. It is explained to her that she was seen using the bag and that she cannot return used merchandise. She tried to argue but was still denied the return. On another occasion she came in tried on bracelets, chose two bracelets and did not have money for the entire purchase but she had her husband's credit card which did not have her name nor did they share the same last name and she became irate that we would not finish her transaction. She threw a tantrum and then attempted to return another bracelet she was already wearing, so she was unable to make that return. She continued to tantrum because the associate was protecting the identity of her husband, or whomever the card belonged to. Oh and one more thing, she always leaves the fitting room in the most catastrophic state! Bye-bye, thanks, but no thanks! Very high strung and demanding.

Lesson: Beware of other retail girls. Girls are mean and some will do any and everything to sabotage another business. It's the same story, they are not happy with their lives so they take it out on others. Give her the same customer service you would give to anyone else. Charm her right out the store.

High End Shopper? Not!

A lady comes in with her mother-in-law apparently they're shopping for gifts and also making some returns. The woman stands in line with 30 items in her hand as if she's ready to make a purchase. She was not ready to make her purchase, instead she wanted to check the price on each of the 30 items. As each price was given she and the mother-in-law decided if they wanted to keep it or shake their heads no. She went on to tell the associate, "I like to shop at high-end retail centers. I usually shop over at the Stratford Center but we are in the neighborhood today and now at the outlets shopping for gifts." (*Do you have the 'high end' associates check each price?*) On top of their huge savings, they ask for gift wrap. When told that there is no gift wrap available, they asked for two separate purchases per person and two separate bags to give as gifts. Mind you she stood there the entire time complaining about everything that she could think of and bragging about their socio-economic status. Not sure if she was from the tax bracket she claimed or not. Very loud and obnoxious. Who's next?

Lesson: The best response is to just do your job, smile, and be courteous. Discuss what's there in your store. Do not give her more ideas or agree with the negative comments. She is obviously putting on airs especially in the presence of her mother-in-law.

Asked and Answered … Again.

Customer: "Hi, can you tell me how much this is?"

Associate: "That's $39.99."

Customer: "Are you sure?"

Associate: "Yes, I'm sure."

Customer: "Okay."

Another associate walks by and the same customer asks the same question and the response was: "$39.99."

Customer: "Okay, no more discounts? Is this the final price?"

Other associate: "Yes, it is the final price."

Customer: "Oh, okay."

The blouse was already marked down at least 50%!

Lesson: Be prepared to sound like a broken record. Some people need to hear the same thing a thousand times before they understand what you mean.

Defective Sunglasses (From A Long Time Ago)

Customer: "We purchased these sunglasses in New York. We don't have the receipt but they're defective" (*What she should have said was that they were slightly bent and worn.*)

Associate: "Sorry, I need to see the receipt"

Customer: "Why can't we just exchange it for another pair?"

Associate: "I need to the exact date of purchase because these sunglasses are from three seasons ago."

Customer: "But I got them last week in your New York store."

Associate: "I understand but I would still need to see a receipt"

Customer: "Never mind." Storms out of the store with teenage daughter.

Associate: "Sorry Ma'am."

How many free pairs of glasses can you get per year? Not on my shift lady.

Lesson: Stick to the return policy. Remain firm yet polite. Maintain good posture but don't be intimidating, i.e. Hands on hips, deep sigh, tight lips, etc.

Price Adjustment: Nail Salon

An older gentleman, around 60 or so, walks in to a nail salon talking on phone. One of the technicians asked, "Can I help you? The gentleman gets off the phone and walks towards the technician (young lady) and begins to whisper loudly to her stating, "I need a manicure but I was here three weeks ago and she didn't cut my nails too well and I was wondering if you would give me a price adjustment by taking off a portion of today's service?"

The technician asked the gentleman to have a seat and someone will be right with him. As he is waiting, he decides to make a few phone calls. The first call was to his accountant and he informed her that he would be out of town for three weeks. Assuming she asked, "Where are you going?" He stated he was going to Greece. Yes, going to Greece as he sat there complaining about $5-$10 price adjustment. A few seconds later we realized exactly how cheap he is because he continues his conversation with a chuckle and says, "You wanna go with me? I can fit you in my luggage." After that comment, we can expect him to ask for a price adjustment from three weeks ago. Meanwhile, the technician walks over to tell him that the manager is not available to approve any price adjustments from three weeks ago. He continued to ask for a discount on his current service. Go figure.

Lesson: Post your policy for price adjustments where all customers can see. Stick by the policy and make sure you leave the salon happy.

BOGO: Buy 1, Get 1 50 % OFF

On a Tuesday afternoon, a customer comes in stating that she was in the store on the previous Friday night. On that day, there was a buy one- get one promotion. She claims that she did not have time to shop but would like to be offered the same promotion that was offered on Friday when she purchased a blouse. There was a promotion on the blouses but she only got one because she was in such a hurry to get to Walleyland she didn't have time to look for another blouse. Hence the reason why she's in on Tuesday to pick out another blouse. The associate explained that you cannot go back and retroactively apply a promotion. Being over 60, the customer felt the need to be very persistent in insisting that she be honored that promotion because she had to go to Walleyland and didn't have time to shop. A bit cranky for someone who just returned from a visit at one of the happiest places on Earth. A manager approved the transaction and the lady was happy.

Lesson: Another high strung lady. Seek a manager to approve the exchange. Everything made sense in her head. Pick your battles, this isn't one you are likely to win.

The Pretender

A customer walks in.

Associate: "Hi, how can I help you?"

No response.

Associate: "Hi, how are you?"

No response. Obviously has a question because she keeps looking up at me.

Another customer enters.

Associate: "Hi, how are you?

Other customer: "Good, thank you."

Associate: "Let me tell you what our discounts are today."

Other customer: "Thank you for telling me."

The other lady comes around the corner and now she's ready to talk and not ignore the associate.

Original customer: "Did you say these are 30% off today?"

Associate: (*Now you want to talk.*) "Yes, they are 30% off today."

Just keep smiling. Just keep smiling. Just keep smiling.

Lesson: Don't take this personally. Just be the source of information and move on with your day.

My Husband Didn't Like It

Associate: "Oh, what's the reason for this return?"

Customer: "My husband didn't like it"

Associate: (thinks) *Biggest pet peeve in the 21st century. Women's lib movement takes a few steps back for each of these situations.*

Associate: (says) "Oh, your husband didn't like it? I have this same dress and it is fabulous! Do you like it?"

Customer: "Yes, I liked it but he didn't like it"

Associate: (thinks) *It's not like he has to wear it.*

Associate: (says) "Well, maybe next time."

Lesson: Don't argue with a customer about political ideas. Smile and make the return. You cannot change the world in one day.

My Kids Didn't Like It

Associate: "Oh, what's the reason for this return?"

Customer: "Yeah, my kids didn't like it."

(*Are your kids paying your bills?*)

Lesson: Most returns require a reason (helps product development). Just put "didn't like it" Most customers don't know "Husband/kids didn't like" isn't an option on the list of reasons for returns.

Got News?

That one time the local news journalist asked for several discounts in ten minutes. The journalist asked the associates several times if there were any additional discounts and was told no. The news journalist requested to speak with manager. Manger responded to the inquiry and explained to the journalist that there were no additional promotions on the item in question. Manager realized what station the journalist was from and proceeded to tell her how well the dress would look on television. The journalist agreed and persisted in asking for more discounts. The manager continued with the same response. The journalist continued to ask if there was a special coupon. Manager offered to open a store credit card to receive an additional discount upon approval, but that was all unless she was a teacher. Journalist declined offers and the dress, then left the store. The evening news had no expose' on "special retail discounts," What was really the point of that visit?

Lesson: Be careful of what you share with strangers. Always refer to media guidelines.

Got News too?

That one time the other news journalist came in and tried on two sweaters. She put one sweater back but tried to negotiate a 'special' discount for the two sweaters. News flash, one can get into trouble for breaking policy and what kind of integrity is that?

Lesson: Never allow yourself to be manipulated into offering special discounts. Redirect this customer to an item that is on a promotion. Make some suggestions but do not offer something the store isn't honoring.

Got More News!

The other time the same journalist from the first scenario came into another retailer and asked for more discounts on top of the current sale price and discount. The journalist requested to speak to the manager. The manager was asked about "hidden promotions" the manager informed the journalist that there were no hidden promotions. The manager offered to take down her information and the store will contact her for special events and sales. The journalist declined the offer and left the store. That's a wrap. On to the next story.

Lesson: Treat local celebrities like regular customers. Don't allow journalists to manipulate you into offering deals that don't exist. Refer the journalist to your manager.

Husband Bully

A lady enters the store with a gift box and gold dress inside (from the holidays). It is now March. She presents the original receipt which was more than thirty days past the 90 day policy. The policy was explained to her and it was also highlighted on the receipt. She claims it was a gift that wasn't given and she can't fit the dress. The policy was repeated to her and she was told there was nothing that can be done at this time for her. A few suggestions were given to her as to what to do with the dress.: donate to a charity, give to a friend, give to a friend's daughter, etc. She was frustrated and left the store.

An hour later she returns with her husband and he demands to speak with a manager and begins to ask, "Why couldn't my wife return this item?" The return policy was explained to him in the same manner it was explained to his wife. He continued to debate the language written on the receipt. In other words, he appeared to have a command of the English language and attempted to find a loop hole in the policy. The manager also had a command of the English language as well and continued to explain the policy to the woman's husband. The man began to talk loud and demand the manager's name and for her to complete the return. He tried to intimidate the manager by staring harshly at her and she met his stare with the same intensity. The manager refused to give her name (safety reasons) and he then began to tell her that she was afraid of getting in trouble. He was told that was not the case, it was a matter of privacy and the company policy does not require associates to give their names to customers. Another example of the Women's Lib movement taking a few steps back – she couldn't have it her way so she brought her big, bad, and entitled husband in to bully a sales associate and manager (a failed attempt) for a return that she had no right to return in the first place. That wife lost respect.

***Lesson*:** Companies need to provide more support to employees when these situations occur. Associates and managers should know the policy and what rights they have for situations such as this. A policy should be in place to collect information from customers to file a harassment complaint. The situation is daunting and mentally exhausting for associates and managers. Just remember to keep your cool, know your rights and fall back on company policy when in doubt.

If I Buy Three Pairs Do I Get A Discount?

Customer: "Hi. If I buy three pairs, is there a discount?"

Associate: "No, we don't have a promotion on the pants today."

Customer: "Even if I purchase three pairs?"

Associate: "Sorry, but we don't have a promotion on the pants."

Customer: "So, there's no discount if you buy more than two?"

Associate: "No, Ma'am."

Customer walks out of store.

Lesson: Maintain your composure. You simply cannot convert all customers to a sale.

Hawaii 5-0

The Hawaii 5-0 girl was the special type. By special, the type that may have missed her medication that day. Hawaii visited the store on several different occasions and on each visit she left an imprint in your memory bank. On this particular day, the store was hosting an in-store event which was invite-only. Hawaii arrived about five minutes after the event started and browsed around. She admired a few items and was in awe and captivated by the presence of an associate that she thought was beautiful. Hawaii was beginning to speak in a very loud and hyper tone as she piled compliment upon compliment to the associate that enamored Hawaii.

Hawaii then inquired about the table set up with refreshments. The associate she was infatuated with explained that the event was by invite and she was welcomed to leave her information so that she can be invited to the next party. Meanwhile, the invited guests continued mingling with the hostess of the event. As Hawaii, continued with her parade around the store, she worked her way towards the event table. Hawaii asked the hostess what was going on. The hostess shared info and exclaimed how glad she was to have her contact information for the next event.

Hawaii proceeded by snatching the guest list and yelled out as she pointed to the list, "I'm Rebecca's guest! See, its right here!" Stunned by this outburst, the hostess was speechless and the other guests were shocked. The store went silent. Hawaii quickly grabbed a handful of cookies and placed them on the plate she had been holding. Hawaii then backed away from refreshment table and headed towards the door. As she walks past the associate she was enamored with, she quietly called her a 'bitch." Hawaii is moving pretty fast at this point because the manager says, "Excuse me?" and expected an apology or some type of explanation to this sudden switch up. Hawaii was on an unapologetic frenzy. Hawaii is now at the door and as she brushes the door frame, threw her free arm in the air and she yells back at her audience, "Hawaii 5-0 Motherfuckers!"

***Lesson*:** Be prepared for individuals that appear to be unstable. Pay attention to body language and voice inflection. Use five words or less. Anything more may agitate or confuse the individual. Bear in mind, they are not mean but at times misunderstood. You can make or break the experience by the words you choose. In some cases, call security. Companies should provide some type of professional meeting or debriefing when these incidents occur; either to the district manager or the team.

6 Weeks Not Pregnant

The lady who was six weeks pregnant, but not really. A lady comes in the store and she's in a hurry. We'll call her Sally. Sally was carrying a bag from Newman Mayfield, hair in two pigtails and she was wearing a t-shirt and jeans. Sally begins to explain that she was looking for something to wear to a financial aid interview at a nearby university (*Financial aid interview?*). Sally came in immediately after the store opened therefore, she had the associate's undivided attention. The associate showed Sally several different pieces to mix and match that would be appropriate for an interview. The associate offered to start a fitting room for Sally but she immediately declined with an intense stare, stating she would like to place the items on hold because she was six weeks pregnant and needed to get something to eat. The associate understood and placed the items in the holding area. Sally said she will return in thirty minutes to try the items. Sally did not return to the store that day as promised but she did return a couple of months later. Upon Sally's arrival, she was greeted and asked about her interview and how her pregnancy was going. Sally stated she didn't have an interview nor was she ever pregnant and that the associate must have mistaken her for someone else. Weird.

Lesson: You win some, you lose some. Don't take it personal or doubt your memory. Some customers like to play mind games.

Oops

"My daughter had a nosebleed and got blood everywhere including these expensive shorts."

Ideally, that is what a considerate customer would have done. However, the bloody mess was not discovered until after the party quickly headed towards the exit. That's okay, we like cleaning up bodily fluids. I guess cleaning bio hazardous waste is in the job description under, "additional" duties. Gross and inconsiderate. Clean up after your own children or at least have the courtesy to tell the employees.

Lesson: When you see a customer racing towards the door with no explanation, know that there's a mess in the room or they stole something. Don't chase after the customer but follow up the situation immediately by checking the store.

Oopsie, poopsie!

"Did my dog just poop on your rug as we're exiting the store? Uh-oh, we'd better run the employees are walking towards the door." All of the employees shook their heads in disbelief and contempt towards the pet's owner. Meanwhile, another customer entering stepped in the poop and now there are poop prints throughout the store. Yay, more bio hazardous waste to clean up. Woof, woof!

Lesson: If you work in a store in which dogs may be allowed, carry doggie bags in your pockets to pick up poop immediately to prevent footprints of poop throughout the store. Pet owners should clean up after their pets. Shame on them ... but you got this!

Oopsie Pee-pee

"Did my dog just pee on your floor and I neglected to clean it up?" Not only did the owner watch the dog pee on the floor but the owner also neglected to offer assistance in cleaning up the pee. Instead, the owner made eye contact with the manager and said, "Sorry, but I gotta go." Really? Now you have to go? I hope your day is riddled with the scent of urine.

Lesson: Yes, pet owners shouldn't make others clean up after their pet. It is inconsiderate, but make sure you always have Clorox wipes handy to clean up any pet accidents.

LGBT Community

Every now and then a member of the LGBT community would come into the store to shop. Particularly, crossdressers and transgendered persons. Unfortunately, they often receive poor service because some associates are too focused on how to address them and fear of using the wrong pronoun. Managers need to address this issue right away when they see a customer that is frequently marginalized by society, offering training directly and by example.

The following scenario occurred in an affluent location: Two women walked into the store together looking for perfume. They were greeted and asked what brought them into the store. Their voices were deep and their dresses were beautiful. The manager could see the associates looked uncomfortable. The manager walked up, introduced herself and suggested her favorite perfume. The conversation shifted from perfume to where they had lunch and their plans for the rest of the day. They made their purchase and left the store happy.

***Lesson*:** Most important lesson is to managers who need to train associates to treat everyone the same no matter what. Understanding when to adjust your greeting and demeanor will make a huge difference in customer interaction. As a representative of the company, make the customer feel at ease. Use a little compassion and understand the effort it takes for some individuals to shop outside the home.

Social Integration

Disabled adults are another group that may be mistreated due to lack of awareness and empathy. In some cases individuals shop with a coach or family member to assist them (when needed). However, in other situations the individual may be out alone and will require assistance. One young lady in particular was in a wheelchair and disfigured in her face which made her speech difficult to understand. The associate was uncertain as to how to handle the situation. Thankfully, the manager was standing nearby and quickly stepped in to assist this customer. The customer wanted a few items but required assistance in retrieving her money as well as packing the items in her backpack. The manager was able to assist the customer because she stopped to listen to her words and asked what she would like help with. The customer, no longer frustrated, was able to get her shopping completed.

Lesson: It is very important that customers feel at ease in your store. Listening skills are very important in the above scenario. The young lady was aware of her limitations and needed assistance. You need to understand the needs of your customers beyond the American with Disabilities Act and not be afraid to help customers that look different. Also, don't be afraid to ask for help – after all, that is in part what your managers are there for.

Part 2

The Criminals

<u>Phone Scam</u>

Customer over the phone: "I made a purchase last night and I was given someone else's bags."

Associate: "Oh really? We haven't had anyone report any missing bags or merchandise."

Customer (scammer): "Well, I have two blouses and a pair of pants. I think I have the items that belong to the customer before me."

Associate: "It's impossible for us to give you another customer's items, especially since we don't hand the customers their bags until after the transaction is complete. Also, we would not have helped you until it was your turn. Are you sure you have the right store?"

Scammer: "Yes, I was there last night. I can't bring the items back today because I work in a hospital but maybe tomorrow."

Associate: "okay, well give me your number and I will ask the associate that may have helped you last night"

Phone disconnects.

Lesson: Understand that criminals sit up daily thinking of ways to scam others. Notify your manager if you get a call regarding mistaken bag identity. If you're a manager, stay up-to-date on the loss prevention newsletters as well as doing research yourself. Keep your team informed and aware. Some associates are uncomfortable with providing customer service to these particular customers and require a lot of reassurance and support.

The Lost Bag

Customer walks in and tells the associate his sister left her bag in the store the night before and he was wondering if he can get the items she left behind. *Hmmmn*, your sister left her purchase and you're here to pick it up.

Customer: "Hi, my sister left her bag here last night. She asked me to pick up the items for her."

Associate: "I'm sorry but no one left their bags here last night. Do you have the receipt?"

Customer: "I don't have her receipt."

Associate: "Well, I'm sorry. Maybe she has the wrong store. Do you know what items she left?"

Customer: Walks over near front of store and begins to pull random items. "I think she had these pants (black), this shirt (white), and this jacket (black leather)."

Associate: "Yes, she must have the wrong store because we didn't sell any of those items last night. If you like, I can ring you up for those now since those are the items she's 'missing'?"

Customer: "No, that's okay." Leaves store.

What the gentleman didn't know is that the same associate he spoke with is the same associate that received the weird phone call about the other customer 'accidentally' taking another customer's bag last night.

Lesson: Communicate all weird phone calls and possible scams to your manager and the loss prevention department. This allows everyone to be proactive if such calls should happen again. Never give away merchandise no matter how compelling the story sounds.

Is This Bike For Me?

A guy dressed in a nice suit stood near the entrance of the store and proceeded to just stand there. A few minutes later he started looking at the bikes that were near the store's entrance. A minute later, the guy rode the bike right out of the store. No one was able to catch him. Hope the suit didn't get too sweaty.

Lesson: Don't ever be fooled by a nice suit. Trust your instincts.

Don't Worry, I'll Switch The Tags For You

The thief with a friend in the store. Customer walks to cash register with about fifty miscellaneous items. Ten random items ring up $.99. Hmmmn, she found a lot of clearance items. Cashier noticed everything was ringing up at $.99. Wait one minute. All of these items have the same barcode.

Cashier: "I'm sorry, Ma'am. I need to get a manager."

Customer: "It's okay. I don't need the stuff." She runs out of the store.

Lesson: Pay attention to how your items are scanning and know the price of your merchandise.

Runaway Shoes

The lady that came in to buy a pair of shoes but decided to steal a pair instead. Supervisor chased her outside to her car, told lady the police were on their way. Lady offers to purchase shoes but supervisor just asked for the shoes back. The supervisor told the lady she will probably be stopped on the freeway.

***Lesson*:** Never chase a thief, it can be a potentially dangerous situation. Your life is more valuable than the shoes. Nevertheless, the threat of being stopped on the freeway was pretty funny.

My Money Is Funny

The guy with the counterfeit traveler's checks. A guy came in to purchase shoes and decided to get a pair. The total came up to about $100 and he provides a check for $500. The cashier had to call for approval but in the meantime she checked the validity and it appeared to be counterfeit. Cashier told the guy she waiting for approval. He didn't have time to wait so he left in what appeared to be a taxi that was waiting. Just walked right out and left his check. Days later the police came in asking questions about some men trying to use counterfeit traveler's checks.

Lesson: Know what traveler's checks look like and share the info with neighboring merchants or mall security.

Authorization Not Approved

A guy walks in and makes a bee line to a particular area in the store. Was greeted by associate but didn't need any help, which is odd because most men that shop in a store for women either need help or they come with a note. This guy appeared to be scared because he kept looking back at the associate. At this point, the associate walks toward him to see if he needed assistance. The gentleman stated he didn't need any help and had made a selection. The associate wrapped the items and then collected payment. The gentleman presented a credit card that wouldn't scan but he insisted the cashier was sliding it the wrong way. Then he used the famous line that credit card thieves use, "Can you just type in the numbers?"

Sales Associate: "No, sir."

Customer/Thief: "I know there's money on the card."

Sales Associate: "Maybe you can call the number on the back of your card?"

Customer: "Yeah, I guess so. I know there's money on there. Can you try it again?"

Sales Associate: "Would you like to use another method of payment?" (Smile.). "I can put the items on hold if you would like to come back?"

He asked the associate where the nearest ATM machine was located and associate provided him with directions. Customer agreed to put items on hold but never returned. Once the customer left, the associate looked up the specific card that was used and found out there were several scams associated with that prepaid credit card. The card was never going to be authorized.

Lesson: Research retail scams before each shift or watch the nightly news. In most cases, the loss prevention department keeps employees in the know of possible scams.

Shoplifting Shop-A-Holics

Two young ladies walk in and head towards the cash register. You can often tell the purpose of the visit by the way a person walks. It's all in the walk.

They had everyone's attention and began to get defensive by saying things like, "What are we ghosts?" "They think we're ghosts." "I think she's prejudiced." After all of the assumptions were made, they were asked by the manager, "How can we help you?"

The girls tried to return jewelry without receipt or tags. They said it was a gift from their aunt. Manager asked if they wanted to wait until their aunt found the receipt so that she can get her money back and not a store credit. The girls rejected that suggestion. The manager figured she would have a little fun with the young ladies. The manager said they had a very generous aunt to gift them a $300 bracelet and several of them! Then, the manager said her aunt is not so generous because she kept receipt forever just in case you have to return a gift.

Manager asked several times if they were sure if they really wanted to return the beautiful bracelets. Again, the young ladies insisted on the return. But then the manager realized that the items didn't have the tags and would need a receipt to process the return. The manager encouraged the ladies to come back once they got the receipt. The young ladies left with all of their bracelets.

The next day, the young ladies appeared with a gift receipt somehow with the current date from another store just hours prior to their visit. Luckily, the same manager was present. Small talk was exchanged. Return processed and then the ladies pulled out several headbands, all of them the same and asked to return them. Unfortunately, the tags were attached and manager had to return all 18 headbands. Wow! The same young ladies sent their mentally disabled sister in to return other "purchases," the sister didn't have a clue and had a difficult time sticking to the script that was prepared for her. The sisters failed to propose other possible scenarios. Just cruel humans (sisters).

Lesson: Customer service. If the ladies were given great customer service and attention, they wouldn't have had the opportunity to take from the same store twice. However, their actions caused their insider from the other store to be fired. The manager took down information from their lovely gift receipt and called the store it came from and inquired about the bracelets and headbands. Lo and behold all of the items were taken from that particular location and they had the help of another employee. It's not worth your credibility or future employment endeavors. Managers should always be on their A-game and quick to think.

Baby, Don't Cry

The girls that would try to steal while carrying a fake baby. The fake baby was ugly. She really tried to work the baby situation. Prior to the "baby" being born, the same girl would come in with a fake belly (guessing to stuff merchandise in her "belly).

Lesson*:* In this situation, a lot of small talk like, "When are you due?" "O-M-G, I can't imagine having a baby!" or "What's it like." If she was truly pregnant, she would have asked for the nearest restroom. Nothing to really learn here except pay close attention to everyone and everything. Shoplifters will try anything and everything.

The worst gift ever

The girl that steals a size zero but she's a size eight. When she came back to return the dress without a receipt, she just said it was a gift. Yes, a 'gift'. Same lady with the fake baby.

Lesson: Recognize your frequent shoplifters and kill them with kindness.

But it has a tag

The lady that tries to return items that are not from the store. This lady rips the tags off of new merchandise and attaches the tag to something old inside of her purse. After the switch-a-roo, she waltzed to the counter to return the items. Not too clever. Boring. It's stealing!

Lesson: Know the merchandise you are selling and beware of these people. The customer may become indignant and is definitely a situation for the manager.

Part 3

The Sales Associates

How Much Are You Spending

The associate who will only speak to a customer that's holding a garment. Anyone else in her opinion is a waste of time. This particular associate isn't into greeting or selling unless you show some interest. (*Why wasn't she let go for her "outgoing" personality?*) To her advantage, she's great at folding. Just keep folding. Just keep folding. Just keep folding.

Lesson: Recognize that managers make decisions for various reasons that you may not understand or agree with. All you can do is your job and not second guess theirs. If the behavior of fellow associates gets out of hand, maybe have a talk with your manager. Subsequently, the manager will have a lot of public relation issues to deal with as a result of the said associate's behavior.

Huh?

The associate who claims to understand the words that are coming out of your mouth; however, when asked a question for clarification, the response is the "deer in the headlights" glare. Really? Retail is not rocket science. You don't even have to do math, calculators are available. That said, you should be able to mentally calculate percentages like, 50% and 10% off of a purchase to quickly assist customers. But, if you can't at least operate a calculator, then there is a problem.

Lesson: Know your own limits and recognize others have limits too. Most managers are aware and will make a cheat sheet with percentages/price points after the discount. Maybe offer help to a co-worker in return for help from them – then both of you enhance your abilities.

Sweet Like Candy

The associate who is so nice they appear like a statue in a wax museum, permanent smile (*full of you know what, or high*) and fluffy words sweet enough to hurt your ears after a six hour shift.

Lesson: Remember, it could be worse – they could be nasty, in so many different ways. Just go with it and smile back. Enjoy the sweetness.

Pee Time?

The associate who takes several bathroom breaks when it's time to do real work. What is this, first grade? Unless clearly pregnant, running to the bathroom constantly is not going to help anyone get their work done, right?

Lesson: In truth, there are many medical reasons that could lead someone to visit the bathroom often. Try not to assume they are using the bathroom for other reasons. Let your manager know of the seemingly excessive use and let them handle it. Then, do your job with a smile, even with the disappearing pee-ster.

How Does This Work Again?

The associate who cannot comprehend the functionality of a cash register but is always the first one trying to ring up the next customer. You give the benefit of the doubt and lo and behold, they are calling you for help. Just keep smiling, just keep smiling, just keep smiling. Politely say, "Okay, these things happen." (*Actually, it only happens to you.*) Now, you're the one full of you know what.

Lesson: Again remember, people have their limits. Maybe talk to your manager about this co-worker only assisting customers on the floor rather than use the register until they have it down a bit better – feel free to offer to help. Teamwork is a good thing.

I See People

The associate who claims they can't handle being around people. *Hmmn*, why are you working in retail?

Lesson: Refer this one to your manager. It is above your pay grade. Understand the manager is aware of the mistake.

Too Hot!

The associate who thinks their style is the $#!%. Nothing further is needed on this one.

Lesson: Make sure the customer is happy and the rest doesn't matter. Refer this one to your manager if you're feeling style-shamed.

Focus!

The associate who has a slight case of OCD so when you assign a task, consider it done!

Lesson: Don't take advantage though. Be sure to do your own work and/or delegate fairly to all employees.

Break Time

The associate who requests a break after working for one hour and then asks to go home early. Take an extended break and just stay home! This is possibly (likely) the same associate who requests frequent bathroom breaks. What is in that bathroom?

Lesson: Refer this one to your manager. It is above your pay grade. Managers, it's time to have a one-on-one. The associate is obviously not happy and may need to set some clear career goals.

Rain Or Shine. Not!

The associate who didn't show up to work because it was raining and she didn't have an umbrella. This incident was quite funny and juvenile. Thank God she usually was a good employee and cute.

Lesson: Don't rely on your good looks and always check the weather as you prepare for your day.

Sale Stealer

The associate who takes your sale right in front of your face and looks you dead in the eyes as the horrible offense is occurring. Just keep cool, just keep cool, and just keep your cool. FYI, the sale-thief was fired the next day for that poor attempt of sabotage. The jokes on you, Biaaaatch!

Lesson: Calmly walk away and go to your manager immediately. It's the manager's job to know what is going on at all times and more than likely they will know the customer you helped. Do the right thing, even when others don't. Karma will work itself out.

'Cause I'm Bossy

The associate who claims they are being bossed around while the other associates are claiming the claimer is the bossy one. Ha, ha, try keeping up. And bossy can also be a negative Nancy at times.

Lesson: Know your role and responsibilities. At times, an associate can say things to their peers that managers can only dream about. If there is a need to be assertive, do so. If the problem persists, go to your manager.

Too Soon?

The associate who thinks promotion means screwing the boss. In actuality, all it meant was different shifts and hours with them because they were done seeing you so much. What's a person to do in a situation like this, get another job, that's what!

Lesson: No idea what to say…Never mix business with pleasure in retail. It will bite you later. Keep your social media out of your work.

Sure, I'll Take Your Worn Items

The associate who can't say NO.

Customer: "I wore this and stained it but it's defective. Can I return it?"

The associate responds with, "ahhh. yeah, sure." What just happened here?

Lesson: Once the customer is gone, politely remind your co-worker of the store's policy regarding returns. If it keeps happening – you guessed it – let your manager handle it. You have done your part.

I'm Bitter and I Want Everyone Else To Suffer

The associate that hates her job but never quits. She complains about the quality of the brand and treatment by upper management. This is the same associate that will only speak to customers holding merchandise. Just keep folding. And smile – always smile.

Lesson: Smile and do your job. Usually, if you ignore the behavior, the perpetrator will stop bringing the negativity to you. They just want a response but don't buy into the shenanigans. Otherwise, refer to your manager if there is a problem (*yes, this is a go to action*). Smile. Smile. Smile.

Don't Hire Me

The associate who walks in from another retailer and complains about her manager and the company. (*You agree with her manager 100%, but just keep squinting while she talks, hoping she doesn't ask for an application*).

Lesson: The writing is on the wall – this person doesn't know how to work in retail and you should do whatever you can, without lying, to prevent them from working with you. If she does ask for that application, simply let her know she can apply online, which is absolutely true. She may forget to apply.

I See Disability Checks

The associate that tried to work up a Worker's Comp case. First, she didn't show up for her scheduled shifts. Second, when she finally called, she was only calling to quit. Her resignation was accepted. Two days later she called back and asked if she was on the schedule but was reminded that she had quit two days prior. She said she wanted to take back the resignation. Two days later a gentleman appears from Worker's Comp department and wanted to discuss the alleged discrimination towards the associate. She didn't win. A year later she came to visit and see how everyone was doing and how much she missed everyone. By the way, not that it matters but all of those accused of discrimination were minorities. Crazy.

Lesson: Things may appear to be chaotic because some associates do gossip, but remember to keep doing your job the right way – even and especially when no one is watching. Everything is being handled by your manager and he/she can't give you the details. Make sure you are being helpful and not a hindrance.

I See Working People

The associate that faked fainting and attempted to fall out on the floor to get a worker's comp case going. Luckily, there happened to be another associate that was certified in first aid and helped to prevent her from any injuries. Later the associate returned with a doctor's note only allowing her to work four hour shifts. A week later the associate resigned. The associate called out sick on her last shift but somehow felt good enough to make an employee purchase on the same day. This is when you demand a parent/associate conference. Something obviously was missed in the upbringing. Oh, yeah, she also got a full-time position two weeks later at another retailer. I wonder how the worker's comp case is working out for her there.

Lesson: There is never a need to fake a doctor's note or a health issue in retail. Just turn in your notice and all will be fine. No hard feelings. Just remember that worker's compensation auditors are thorough and see fraudulent claims a mile away.

The Coffee Run

The associate that told the new manager that the morning routine was to clock-in first and then go get coffee. The new manager already had her coffee so she politely told the associate that was not a routine she was going to abide by. The manager told the associate that she may use her 10 minute break within the first hour if time permits to get coffee. The associate was not happy. As a matter of fact, she was never happy about much after that. Nice try but the <u>Dennis the Menace</u> antics only works on rookies.

Lesson: Do your job. That's it ... just do your job. Don't waste your time trying to convince a new person, especially another manager to break the rules to suit your personal needs. Clearly, a manager will not (should not) take the bait. Similar to *The Parent Trap.*

<u>I'm Tired</u>

The associate that walked off the sales floor to

get things and go home because she was "tired"

One associate had about 15 minutes left on her shift and was given a task she decided not to finish. Instead, the task did do was to go grab her items and come out to the floor as if it were time for her to go home. When she came back she was asked, "Where were you?" she said, "I just went to get my stuff." Still puzzled (*obviously, didn't ask the right questions*) the other associate asked, "Why?" She said, "Well, I'm tired and I want to go home." Too stunned to come up with anything else that wouldn't get her fired, the senior associate agreed with her. It was time for her to go home. And that was her last shift.

Lesson: Always check in with your manager or supervisor prior to shift ending. Work is work. You will get tired. Just know this going in. But smile and do your job – it will pay off in the long run.

Every Weekend Please

"My availability is only on the weekends but can I have every weekend off?" Like, why are you here and why are you wasting both of our time?

Lesson: Don't be this associate. Just quit and give someone else an opportunity to have your job. Refer to manager. Refer to manager. Refer … Oh, you get it.

I Quit

The associate that quit because she wanted to sleep-in on one particular Sunday instead of attending a mandatory store meeting before Black Friday.

Lesson: You still have your job. And now a chance at more hours. Understand that meetings are scheduled for a reason and it's important for your success to attend. It may seem mundane and you think you know everything but important information about the company and your store will be discussed as well as holiday procedures. Don't be the associate that misses the meeting and come back clueless. Managers get to see who is invested and ready for the next step.

No-Show To A Shift

I'm not going to show up to work because I asked for this day off. The day off was never approved; it was just a request. However, some associates don't understand the difference between a request and an approval. This is where Whine-o'clock hour begins.

Lesson: You must have prior approval or it will be considered a no-show. Do your job and trust that the manager has this one handled. Make sure you have a copy of the schedule indicating that your request was approved.

Dress Code Issues

The associate that threw a tantrum because she was reminded that the she was out of dress code. Five minutes after Whine-o'clock. This was a three hour tantrum. Not getting paid to do what the parents should have done years ago.

Lesson: Know the dress code, follow it. It really is that simple.

I Can't Come In, I Was In An Accident

The associate that lied about being in a car accident on the way to work. Associate said she was waiting for Highway Patrol to arrive. Manager asked if she was okay and to call when she was on her way. Something didn't add up. Manager called local Police Department and Highway Patrol but no accidents were reported for that day. Associate was asked to bring in a Police report but she said there was no report because she didn't call the police. Ha, ha, what a terrible web she weaved.

The same associate from the above scenario sent her mother in to return an item (*by the way, the associate was no longer employed at this location*). When asked if she had a daughter that was a former employee, the mother stated, "No, you must be thinking of someone else." No wonder the associate could lie so easily. She got it from her momma.

Lesson: Always be honest. Lies find a way to trap you. Although, the mother could have been embarrassed by her daughter's behavior and didn't want to admit that her daughter worked there.

<u>It's Always Time For A Break</u>

The associate who thought she should sit in the fitting rooms while working and send text messages from her phone. Strike one.

Still on break? The associate was caught sitting in the messy fitting rooms while on the clock during holiday rush. Strike two.

"But I'm waiting for a text"

The associate appeared to not understand the cell phone rule of not having it on the sales floor, which included her pants pockets. Strike three.

Lesson: Follow the rules. They are there for a reason – to ensure jobs are performed and customers are given appropriate attention. The text can wait.

Is All Of This For Me?

The seasonal associate that thought half of the left-overs from the company's sponsored lunch should go home with her. Too many strikes.

Lesson: It isn't necessarily wrong for her to want to take some food as leftovers, but all of it? Remember to share – and check with your manager about the amount that might be appropriate, if any.

Clean?

The associate that was proud about not knowing how to clean a bathroom. Another great parenting moment. Pathetic and not cute.

Lesson: Can you say "Manager"? Perhaps a parent/manager conference would be better yet inappropriate.

It's My Unique Style

The associate that said they like fashion but wanted to advocate on wearing out of season attire and funny looking shoes. (*Please, go and watch <u>The Devil Wears Prada</u> and get a clue.*)

Lesson: Dress the part! Do not work in fashion forward environment and not be wearing the current fashion or anything; and don't go on and on about skills you don't have unless you can back it up with action (*or fashionable attire*).

I Can Sell!

The associate that called HR when asked about their sales goals from a manager.

Lesson: Know who handles what within the company and follow the appropriate chain of command or maintain your goals and ask for help when you are not meeting the expectations. A good manager will discuss your progress and opportunities on a weekly basis.

The Art of Time Management

The holidays are the worst for customers and associates alike. The customers are always wanting more time in a day to do the things they have been putting off for months. They come in with three kids pushing a stroller and need an entire wardrobe with only ten minutes to shop. The pressure is on the associate to show her at least three fabulous outfits and guess her size. Meanwhile, the kids are bored and baby is ready for its next feeding. The associates are ready to leave and go home. Plan accordingly.

Lesson: Know your products, then you can get this customer, and her kids, in and out in a flash. Always, always have two outfits ready to go for two occasions: Work and after work. It would also be great if the chosen pieces worked like a two for one. For instance, a black dress and blazer for work with a nice statement necklace to add and ditch the blazer for after work. Win-win for all involved.

The Know-It-All 18 Year Olds

Some of these children, called children because that is how they behave. Learned to be disrespectful in the work place towards their superiors and elders. (*Who knows where they learned the behavior?*) If only a report card could be sent home to their parents regarding their job performance, it might not be so cute and funny then. It's sad how one wanna-be can spoil someone with so much potential.

Really, this associate type is at the crossroads where the entitled meets the attention seeker and people pleaser. The people pleaser is so caught up in sucking up to the entitled prick that they can't see past the bad job performances. The entitled is so caught up in the smell of their own asses to the point where their poor performance comes as a shock to them with an "air" of "it's not my fault" my favorite with the know-it-alls, is the understanding of the job description. Can you do A, B, and C and at times D? Response, oh yes I can't wait to do A, B, and C. In theory it sounded like a wonderful and meaningful experience but in practice it was more foreign than a Canadian penny.

Lesson: Don't say you know something if you don't … really, say what you know, then back it up with action. Some managers will be happy to train you but don't lie or allow others to hinder your progress.

Lazy. Lazy

The representative came to the interview, but the lazy young adult is who actually showed up to work with one main goal: look cute. This associate thinks the sales just fall out the sky and maids come to clean the store. In all places of employment, beyond the actual job, employees are expected to clean up after oneself and in some cases, it's a specific job duty. Cleaning duties may include the simple task of throwing away your trash, making sure paper towels make it to the garbage, and scrubbing the toilet. Believe it or not the entitled and lazy adult don't know how to clean nor do they think it's their responsibility to clean. Not sure who to blame, the parents or the "know-it-alls" from above.

***Lesson*:** Learn how to clean up after yourself. No one wants to work with a slob. Ask for help if you are unsure but don't sign off on a task as completed if it isn't.

Up-Sell Problem

T'was Christmas Eve and some customers just left work with just enough time to squeeze in some last-minute shopping. After being on their feet for eight hours they were extremely exhausted and wanted to get home, but stopped to grab a small stocking stuffer for someone special. For one customer, on the menu: a single gift card.

The associate at the counter wanted to up-sell the customer, who had to repeatedly tell her no thank you. The associate continued to tell the customer about the benefits she was missing out on. The customer told her she understood that and that it was a great deal, but not at this time. The associate continued to push the deal, she just kept asking and asking and asking! The customer just kept asking and asking and asking if she could just have the gift card that she chose to purchase? The associate continued trying to up-sell the deal that she was offering.

Finally, the customer had enough, turned and said, "Never mind!" She walked right out the door with the associate screaming after her, "Please wait everything is ready! I already scanned it! Please, wait it's ready you can buy it!" The customer said "never mind, you lose!" Mind you, there was a line going out the door and this girl did not have the time for her unnecessary persistence. There's a time and a place and you have to know when to listen to your customer during an up-sell attempt.

Lesson: There is a fine line between up-selling and losing your customer. Rule of thumb: if a customer has rejected your suggestions three times, leave it alone. Continue with the items or requests already expressed. If you don't follow the rule above, you will create an uncomfortable situation for yourself and the customer. The customer may not want to shop with you or the retailer again. Know your boundaries. And definitely don't go running after to the customer to try to save the sale.

To Up-sell or Not!

In the culture of selling (professionally), associates are taught to up-sell, to entice the customer into spending more money, either leaving with two items or one item with the highest price point. The metrics are calculated within a special system that identifies the salesperson, amount spent and number of items. The metrics measure not only the associate's performance but the store's performance as well. Now, with an understanding of how most retailers work, you will understand the situation below and how the associate could have created a win-win for herself and closed the sale much sooner.

The location was at a prestigious shopping center located in an affluent area. The assumption is that every customer can afford everything they touch. The thing is, just because one can afford something doesn't mean it should be purchased. One customer moseyed into this plush and proper baby store where headbands started at $30. While browsing and admiring all of the beautiful dresses and fine woven sweaters and cardigans, another customer, a mother, was shopping for her two girls: a two month old and a four year old. The mother was debating between two dresses, one frilly with pink and white stripes in two different sizes and one solid pink dress with a subdued ruffled trim for an infant. The debate took place at the cash register with the associate who needed to decide if she should upsell.

As the original customer was walking by, the mother asked her what she thought about the dresses she had chosen. The question was if the solid pink for the infant would match the pink and white frilly that was intended for the four year old. The real question was if it was appropriate to spend so much on a dress for an infant to only wear once, whereas the pretty pink and subdued was priced a little less that the other frock. The intention was to have the girls in matching dresses. She asked if the pinks in each dress complimented the other. Indeed, the pinks were close enough to wear for a picture. The original customer also explained that a hair accessory could be worn by the infant that accentuates the floral applique on the frilly dress. The woman agreed and she already had something at home to accessorize the baby and both girls would have a new dress. The mother asked the associate what her thoughts were and the associate continued to push for both frilly dresses. The mother was set on the plan the other customer suggested and got the pink, ruffled trimmed dress with a cute headband for the infant and the pink frilly frock for the four year old. The associate was so busy trying to up-sell, she failed to listen to the customer and another customer had to do her job. (*Not good. Not good at all!*)

Lesson: The associate should to listen to what the customer is saying and know when the sale is slipping, don't push for the item the customer is contemplating against. Instead, provide some options for the customer and allow the customer to make an informed choice on their own. Make sure you have other options or suggestions to offer quickly. Doing so, the associate is removed from the decision and the customer is now in control. It's a win-win because you get the two items sold to satisfy the store's goals and the customer is happy. Don't up-sell and lose the sale for pushing too much. Remember, you want the customer to return and trust your opinion on the next visit. And definitely don't let other customers do your job.

Part 4

The Management

<u>The Key holders</u>

Key holders hold a very special position in the store. They have some power but not a lot of power. Some don't understand the boundaries between them and associates. Managing their feelings and their roles is sometimes too difficult for them to provide disciplinary action because they still want to be cool and the associate's favorite supervisors. Further evaluation is necessary for future promotions. Various other types of key holders exist. Let's take a look.

The key holder that added a shift for an associate who was a no-show the day prior. When asked, the key holder denied adding a shift (without manager's approval). The shift was never on the schedule but the associate just happens to show up for the "unknown" shift. This is the same key holder that felt the need to be liked by all of the associates. That key holder is still waiting to be promoted to the next level.

The key holder that was friends with all of the associates and undermined the authority of other managers. She is still looking for that promotion.

The key holder that hid in the stockroom from a customer because she put the customer's hold back out onto the sales floor and someone else purchased the items. The customer came to collect her items but was highly upset and spoke in a disagreeable tone. The key holder was such a wimp! She allowed someone else to clean up her mess. You know what they say, "If you can't take it, go home!"

Dear key holder that can't handle customers:

You are in a position where you have to stand up for what you have done.

Sincerely,

The other managers

The key holder wasn't wrong in putting the items back. The customer had the items on hold for nearly a week and the policy is to only hold items for 24 hours. Clearly, the customer was not right. However, this story brings us back to the entitled customer. This customer always wants to hold merchandise hostage in hopes of the price going down further until she finally decides to show up. She feels entitled to countless perfume samples, bottled water, and ridiculous style finders. She also bully's associates into breaking the rules and policies. Nevertheless, the key holder needed to have a bit more backbone. No respect for her. Next.

The other key holder that lacked backbone and sent her sister (quite hideous sister. She looked like one of Cinderella's stepsisters) into the store in an attempt to bully a manager. Well, the joke was on her because that is reverse harassment. Now that recess is over, the adults can get back to work. Next.

The jealous key holder will also sabotage a plan by calling out sick. Fortunately for her she was somehow able to produce a doctor's note each time. The jealous key holder would also request the same time off that another manager requested off months in advance. She will then throw a tantrum when her time off request was not honored. If her time was not honored she would call out sick and again would produce a doctor's note stating that she was too ill to come in for three days.

The jealous key holder still has some growing up to do. Perhaps, she left home too early or was promoted too soon and is not emotionally prepared for the job description. Instead of learning and observing she chooses to be backstabbing and immature. Her new name should be Whiny Smurf because all it boiled down to be is whining. It was always whine-o'clock for her.

That time the key holder thought she was being sneaky while looking for another job. The key holder forgot to tell the new employer not to come into the store and leave a message regarding her next training opportunity. The key holder appeared to act as if none of it was true. No one cared. Just be honest. Everyone wants to move up. (It did seem weird that a key holder that hid from customers wanted to be the big boss. Delusional.) Next.

Lesson: If you want to be promoted, lead with dignity and by example. Know the rules, follow them, and don't be a broken link in the management chain even if you disagree with your direct supervisor.

The Managers

It's always nice when a new manager comes on board and has no idea on how to run a business. You expect more from someone in a higher position, but it has a lot to do with whoever hired this individual in the first place. When your boss is doubtful of their skills then you know it's time to go. When she asked an associate what to do, that associate simply looked her in her eyes and stated, "You're going to do your job. That's what you're going to do!" And she just stood there staring as if she didn't understand a word that came out of the associate's mouth, who then simply said, "Goodbye and good luck, this is my last day." Three months later the store was in ruins and it hasn't been the same since. The person who hired her was soon let go as well, which explains the trickle-down effect of service and the quality of the individuals that were hired during the era of that manager and district manager.

Lesson: As a manager, you should not apply for a job you are not prepared to handle. It's normal to be nervous but it's very selfish to hold a position that could benefit someone else that's better prepared. Be honest with yourself.

The assistant manager that got her first real opportunity from a very kind and generous store manager that decided to teach her everything she needed to know in order to succeed. Well, it sucks big time when you decide to bite the hand that led you up the ranks. One day, the assistant wasn't feeling warm and fuzzy with her manager, so she decided to call around to other stores and complain to the other store managers. How uncomfortable to hear mean things about your peer. Well, the district manager learned of all of this gossip and told the assistant to stop. The assistant didn't take the district manager seriously and continued to gossip with her manager's peers. At this point, the district manager had enough and called a meeting. The meeting was not warm and fuzzy, it was a moment to hold the gossiper accountable for her actions. No promotions for the gossiper. Next.

The manager that was upset when another manager unfriended her on Facebook. Isn't that the silliest and most juvenile behavior for an adult? Whine o'clock again.

Lesson: Work is work. While relationships build in all sorts of places, remember to stay professional in the work place. Most importantly, know your job. While it is okay to seek help in a new setting, even from subordinates, be sure to get up to speed quickly so you can lead by example and get that next promotion.

Black Friday Management Choices

The day where good sense and manners take a dive! The store team is pumped, energized, and prepared to deal with the most ill-mannered adults. A special holiday meeting was held just for this day. The district manager and anyone ready to score a serious bonus is all of sudden micro-managing to the tenth power. Long hours and hardly no time for family or home life. All of this, to encounter some of the earth's most dreadful personalities. I have never seen so many impatient and spiteful individuals. If you expected to wait in a short line on Black Friday, then you had unrealistic expectations. All of this for a discount on something they will likely return by the first of the month.

Historically, the store never opened at midnight and the clientele never requested it because they are the type of clients that are entertaining their husband's colleague's as well as hosting a gathering. The data was relayed to the new manager that opening at midnight would be a waste of payroll. Since she was under twenty-five, she was apparently still in the, "I know everything phase" and decided to schedule accordingly. Three customers walking through the mall from another store popped in and that was it until 7a.m. Meanwhile, when the manager realized her naiveté, she began calling everyone scheduled after midnight every two hours for updates and moving shifts further into the normal hours of operation. Imagine being scheduled from 12a.m. to 8a.m, this means that you spent half of your Thanksgiving sleeping when you could have been doing something for yourself or spending time with family. This particular case is not the norm but it is something good managers should be cognizant about.

Lesson: Managers should realize that sometimes they have to listen to someone that may have more knowledge than them and not feel threatened. Associates need to understand that at the end of the day, it's the manager's responsibility and they have to answer to their supervisors. Basically, just do your job. If scheduled, show up, be polite, and help your customers best you can, whether 3 or 300.

Facebook "Thank you"

Thank you for following *The Detailz In Retail* on Facebook. Your support is greatly appreciated!

Bernadette, Falawna, Janelle F., Tina Y., Dominique Tatum, Brandi C., Martin Grant, Damain B., Alice B., LaTanya G., Isabella, Marissa H., Andrea F., Tudie F.G., Veronica L., Crissa T., Gingi W., Jaelyn, Tina Y., Sarah J. MichaelAnn M., David C., Eva C., Nicki A., Dessirree C., Sheree C., Jazze, Nova C., Jeany C., Candice R., Wahnly D., Elisabeth L., Michael F., Angela M., Constance B., Rochelle D., Irene H.

ABOUT THE AUTHOR

Markesha G. Tatum has worked in various retail establishments and management for more than twenty years. No matter the product, customers have always presented an interesting challenge to associates. Questions always arose as to the best way to handle this type or that type of person. Through it all, Ms. Tatum sought a manual to give associates and managers new insight into retail customer relations. When none was found, she decided to write her own and <u>The Detailz of Retail</u> was born – written to both educate and entertain.

With this being her first book, Ms. Tatum has plans for additional books, including a follow up to <u>The Detailz of Retail</u>. Ms. Tatum manages her own consulting firm and continues to work retail selling vacation packages. She holds a Bachelor of Arts degree in English Literature with her sights set on a Master's degree at some point in the future. She lives in Northern California with her husband, her teenage daughter, and an eleven month old daughter.

www.ingramcontent.com/pod-product-compliance
Lightning Source LLC
Chambersburg PA
CBHW031355040426
42444CB00005B/298